Release   Renew   Revitalize

A TIMELESS KEEPSAKE

Charisse Marei

I hold in my possession

A Timeless Keepsake

Personalized and secured with my inscription.

I decide when to open, turn, and design the pages.

Introduction

A Timeless Keepsake is designed with you in mind. It's the one place to Release, Renew, Revitalize memories from days gone by, the present, and what is yet to come.

Have you given thought to how to begin the journaling journey? Will you set the stage to set the mood to enlighten and inspire thoughts that will elevate the overall experience? It is when key essentials are in place that the journaling experience blossoms.

In preparation to journal, mindfully seek a special place to fully engage to add substance to your writings. This will lay the foundation to readily tap into inner inspiration with passion and purpose and enhance clarity. These preparatory measures have a tendency to enlighten your being. I believe the energy felt from the surrounding environment nourishes the soul and opens the mind to imprint sparkle and lasting fantastical treasures. Where to journal is a personal preference (PP) and varies with mood. You may choose a private setting at home or a public place—in a cafe, under a tree, on a train, by a body of water.

Use my scenario as a guide. It's a mini version of how I set the stage to journal. Today, I chose to write this message in a familiar environment: my home. To fulfill my journaling awareness, the emphasis is on location, comfort, views, and aromatics.

I clasp the journal close to my chest with arms folded. As I stand in the kitchen my eyes glance to and from a room, a sofa, a chair, and the small upper patio in search of a peaceful place to reflect and write. Today I am drawn into the semi-private room off the kitchen.

In rhythmic repetition, my fingers gingerly tilt the essential oil bottles categorized by type on the three-tier stand. I wonder, *What is the essential oil of choice today?* As I ponder my intention for this journaling journey, I breathe in the aromatic blends of White Angelica, Awaken, and Sacred Mountain.

I grasp Sacred Mountain in my hands with certainty and welcome spiritual connection. I pour a mixture of the oil and water into the water reservoir of a favored diffuser that sits atop a small wood column stand. As the mist releases from the ventilation hole, I mindfully breathe in deep breaths of aromatic purity to nurture self-love, empowerment, and emotional balance.

Before opening the cover page, I take a few more moments to disengage from the business of life. I graciously spritz my journal with Breezy Blossom book spray to manifest inner love. A deep *ahh* is released.

As I sit, my body naturally takes form to the plushness of the chair. It is positioned in front of a window and on a slight angle to enhance interior and occasional exterior views of the meditation garden. "The Girls," Sage and Citrus, my two bichons frises, snuggle atop the throw and place their warm, fluffy bodies next to mine.

There is no one focal point, only vignettes of compositions to mindlessly rest the eye. I notice the whimsical flair of the seven-foot-tall chandelier hanging effortlessly from a triangular box support system, and the curvilinear shapes formed by the hundreds of small, aqua glass balls. My mind wonders, *How is it possible for this sizable fixture to appear unfathomably weightless as it suspends in mid-air?*

I observe the simplistic design of the white wood shutters. They hang with the utmost authority in their elongated form, yet project a natural soothing unity on each of the seven windows. I observe the fluidity of sunlight that flows gingerly through the open slats and into my space. As the warmth of the white light energy encircles my being, I begin to disengage from the busyness of life.

As I sit, external sounds of motors running and birds chirping begin to fade away. The space around me slowly transforms into an airiness of serene silence.

I lift my finely sharpened wood graphite pencil between my fingers. With a slight rotation of my wrist, the pencil gently rests on the middle finger in preparation to make its first mark on the page. With anticipation I envision the sound of the graphite connecting with the paper. What appears is perhaps a mere squiggle of lines or a myriad of inspirational keywords. It's solely a reflection of thoughts stemming from my mind to commence my story. And so I begin.

Infuse this book with positive vibration and beautiful earth energy to enhance the mind, body, and spiritual connection of this journaling experience. For within your hands is the making of a treasure—*A Timeless Keepsake* fashioned with a personalized imprint of life-giving attributes. What you choose is a reflection of your unique personal style.

Feel the energy!

Preparation to Journal

As you begin the journaling journey empower yourself with action-inspiring techniques to enlighten the way. They are the foundational tools to transfer cherished thoughts onto paper with gratifying purpose.

Eco-Reference Checklist—Journaling Essentials

Preparation is key. Gather your ChaCha bag and fill with journaling essentials to keep clutter feelings at bay. Refer to the mini checklist to guide the way. Add personal favorites to the list.

Happy, Healthy Eco-Shopping!

Staple Pieces	Options	Essential Oils
• ChaCha bag	• throw	•
• *The Bathroom* book	• pillow	•
• *A Timeless Keepsake*	• furry friend	•
• charcoal pencils	• diffuser + essential oil (PP)	•
• color pencils	•	•

Staple Pieces	Options	Essential Oils
Breezy Blossom book spray		
ChaCha bracelet		
therapeutic essential oil (PP)		
glass water bottle + essential oil		

The Overall Intention

Set an overall fantastical intention for your new *A Timeless Keepsake* book. Be specific. Embrace its natural splendor with a consciousness to uplift spirits that will guide you forward with love, clarity, and purpose.

- Sit in a seated yoga pose or any comfortable position.
- Lightly spritz the cover and interior pages with Breezy Blossom book spray.
- Close both eyes.
- Gently lift the book up and under both nostrils to breathe in the aromatic splendor.
- Take a slow, deep breath in through the nose and release through your open mouth.

Breathe!

- Give those beautiful arms and hands a little shake and then rest atop each leg or on the arm of the chair.
- Open hands and turn palms to face up.
- Place an overall intention. Visualize the manifestation.

Embrace!

Journal Entry Intentions

Before each journal entry take a few moments to mindfully unveil the one thought inspiring your palette. Does this intention emanate inner and outer love? Is the pencil urging to move across the page in whimsy flair to form one word, one squiggle, at a time?

You decide!

You choose when to transform the blank canvas into a personal story style. Willingly delve into memories from years gone by, tap into the vibe of the present, or imagine what is yet to come. It's a mindfully engaging starting point to express on paper.

Write each story as you see it. As you feel it. Thoughts will crystalize as you become aware, integrating and transforming all that swirls from within to written words, sketches, and illustrations with perhaps a splash of color.

You may laugh, you may cry.
You may embrace, you may share.
It's your journey.

Take notice as the words unify page after page as they reveal stories to capture the soul and imagination. When complete this book becomes a timeless treasure of health-giving qualities handmade with conscious intention.

But you must begin this journaling journey to reap the rewards of each heartfelt story. Tap into inner inspiration to reveal the intricacies and enchantment of whatever captures your being from the inside out and the outside in. After all, you are the designer of your journey and the guardian of your words. You decide when to open and turn the pages.

My wish for you sparkles with everlasting delight.
May *A Timeless Keepsake* naturally interlace with your genuine character and written expression.
May your intentions manifest and inner light shine.

The pages are reserved for you.
Just write.

Treasure Your Book

Love & Light

Charisse Marei

Using *A Timeless Keepsake* -

A Timeless Keepsake is designed to use by itself or alongside One Room at a Time: *The Bathroom.* Each page waits for you—is reserved for you—to place your imprint.

Journal Entry Intentions

Fashion a rhythmic ritual. Begin each journal entry with intention.

Nine key steps to setting an intention:

1	Gather your ChaCha bag.
2	Diffuse a pure essential oil (PP) to enhance the mood and to permeate the breathe-able air.
3	Choose a special place to sit peacefully, get cozy, and breathe deeply.
4	Remove external noise, just for a short time while you write.
5	Place *A Timeless Keepsake* on your lap and spritz with Breezy Blossom book spray.
6	Dab several drops of essential oil over your heart chakra.
7	Take a few moments to transition into relaxation. Permit breath to be center stage. Close your eyes. Set free any wondering thoughts tapping into your consciousness.
8	Slowly, consciously, breathe in deep breaths of inhalation (through your nose), hold, and then exhale (through your mouth). Repeat three times.
9	Place an intention.

The Pages

The pages readily await the release of your inner vision.

Inspirational sayings are sprinkled throughout the pages to encourage heartening thoughts and to raise spirits. They speak to you.

Before turning to the next page, express a line or two of gratitude.

I am grateful . . .

When an inspirational word comes to mind, turn to the last page of the journal. This is the one place to gather and create a personal mini-keyword reference guide of fantastical words. Add each word as it comes to mind—during waking hours and when awakened during sleep.

Transform the pages to suit your personal story style!

Use Alongside The Bathroom Book

Each chapter of *The Bathroom* book commences with a personal story, *My Story*, and relates to the chapter content. At chapter's end it's your turn to present a favorable like-minded story, *Your Story*. Three bullet points are presented as *Thoughts to Guide Your Thinking* and lead into the one question or statement at hand. This is your cue to write your story in these pages.

The Writing Tools

To further enhance the earth-energy connection, I encourage the use of graphite pencils for written words and creative expression. Gather those gorgeous colored pencils to add a splash of color as you see it, as you feel it.

Eco-Tips

A Time to Gather

- Fill this book with mindful treasures.
- Inspirational sayings are interwoven into the pages.
- Glance through the pages when you need a bit of cheering up. A special message will pop to guide the way.
- When in doubt send love.
- Acknowledge life with gratitude.
- Share the journey. Gather with family and friends in the comfort of a living room. Set forth to journal, to engage in the blessings of story-making and story sharing.
- Host a journaling journey meet-up to attract like-minded people.
- Know that within your hands is the making of *A Timeless Keepsake.* A valuable, heartfelt treasure to pass on to a loved one to keep memories alive.

ChaCha

Have you met ChaCha? ChaCha is an extension of me. She manifested through thought, my thought. She is the modern-day representation of a fairy—good-natured, vibrant, and whimsical. Her purpose is to guide you along a personal transformational journey to manifest a fabulous Eco-Conscious, Healthy-Living Lifestyle.

Symbolically, she senses your wish for change and travels effortlessly to your home. She enters in preparation to lift spirits and encourage the change you seek—one step at a time, one room at a time. Your entire being will radiate as you travel the path to Release, Renew, Revitalize.

With this book in hand, you will feel ChaCha's guidance along an awakening path to reflect your new journey. Take delight in her uplifting spirit, for it will inspire lasting change.

ChaCha Bracelet

The ChaCha Bracelet is more than an aesthetically enchanting *au naturel* bracelet. It is a treasure of health-giving attributes and a symbolic representation of your intention. Each precious gem is infused with positive vibration and beautiful earth energy. The joining of the beads is intended to raise your conscious awareness to enhance well-being and soothe your mind.

Gracefully cup the handmade bracelet in both hands.
Visualize your personal intention.
Believe in the manifestation of your intention.
Place the ChaCha bracelet around your wrist.

With purpose, choose a pure essential oil.
Dab on the sea glass pendant supporting the three dangling minis.
Breathe in the aromatic qualities.
Feel your intention begin to blossom.

The trio of dangling ancient Roman glass minis are essential.
They represent the 3Rs.
A vivid reminder to bring forth your intention to

Release, Renew, Revitalize.

With each velvety touch
and mindful glance
your special intention resurfaces.
It speaks to you.

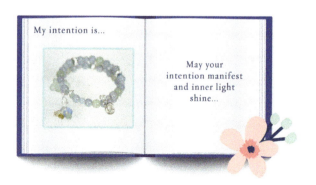

My intention is...

May your
intention manifest
and inner light
shine...

ChaCha Bag

The ChaCha Bag is quite special. You see, it was designed with you in mind. It's a treasure of health-giving attributes—handmade with love, purpose, and eco-chic materials.

Its purpose on the outside is to be seen in a glimpse.
A visual reminder to keep you intentionally moving forward.
To lift spirits.
To Release, Renew, Revitalize.

Its purpose on the inside is to organize the traveling transformational tools in one place.
It's chic and functional.
It speaks to you.

ChaCha Bag

Contents

The Bathroom
A Timeless Keepsake
tablet * USB diffuser *
* pencil * measure * swatches
color cards * water bottle

RELEASE
RENEW
REVITALIZE

A TIMELESS KEEPSAKE

...journey enlightens and inspires me
...ch change, big or small.
...I am aware.
...am ready.

Charisse Marei

www.CHARISSEMAREI.com

PURPOSE

inspire

It all begins with the planting
of a seed!

Release, Renew, Revitalize
with flowing breaths of intention . . .

I am conscious
of the energetic shift
taking place within and around me . . .

I willingly welcome
greater purpose . . .

Sprinkle words
across the page . . .

I feel the urge to send
wishes of pure love
and protection to . . .

As I write,
I discover delight
in each little thought . . .

Transferring thought to paper
provides clarity
concerning the person
I've become . . .

I am encouraged to linger
a bit longer within these pages . . .

I am pulling it all
together with purpose . . .

All things pure are
gorgeously gratifying . . .

My written words are
a reflection of
my unique
story—boundless, subtly changing,
conforming to my imagination . . .

I am inspired by endless words
and thoughts dripping off the paper . . .

RELEASE

I set you free!

believe

*Clutter is anything or anyone that makes me feel
less than the person I am meant to be!*

My creative ideas
flow freely . . .

I believe all things
meant to be
flourish with ease . . .

The transformation of my
thoughts to paper begins
with me, one word at a time . . .

I believe
in me . . .

I am conscious of my thoughts
releasing, stretching boundlessly
beneath the heavenly sky . . .

I am a reflection of
my thoughts (energy) . . .

It's what I do
with my thoughts
that makes all the difference . . .

I believe an awe-inspiring light
shines within to guide me
along a journey of transformation . . .

Release and then celebrate
with joy the gift of life . . .

I believe simplicity
and joyful happenings
are at the helm . . .

A new approach =
a new me . . .

Today, as the day
before, is a gift . . .

RENEW

To give fresh new life!

grow

The transformation of thought to paper
begins with one word at a time!

I am grateful for a new,
crystalized awareness
to further elevate my writings . . .

I tap into the energy
of the environment
to embrace balance and harmony . . .

I am aware of the delight
embracing my being
as memories of you surface . . .

My breath
comes with ease . . .

I am prepared to rediscover
fanciful (remarkable) facts . . .

I consciously choose
what I need.
No less, no more . . .

I willing embrace the aura
of warmth encompassing my being . . .

I trust in the beauty
of whatever lies before me . . .

I am grateful for
my journey of transformation . . .

I am conscious of
my thoughts—I reflect, I smile . . .

I am conscious of
my creative side
awakening, flourishing . . .

It's how I nurture my thoughts
that makes all the difference . . .

REVITALIZE

I welcome new life!

beauty

*I am peaceful, inspired, energetic, and beautiful from
the inside out and the outside in!*

I am conscious of
the light radiating
from within . . .

I believe in a graceful,
visual transition . . .

My aura beams with beautiful color
extending far beyond
my physical stature . . .

The sweet scent blowing through
the atmosphere remains as a
majestic imprint in my being . . .

I take pleasure in
my awakening path,
a reflection of
a new journey . . .

I am enveloped in a reflection of bliss
emanating from my eco-consciousness . . .

The 3Rs: a gentle reminder
to move forward with
mindfulness . . .

I enjoy a splash of color
for it adds sparkle
to my day . . .

Sparkling light dances
around me,
through me,
within me . . .

As I mindfully gaze
into a thought, a blissful
memory surfaces . . .

I am on a personal journey to
embrace mindful changes
that will enrich my life . . .

I foster pleasurable thoughts
as I write about . . .

Enfold in rhythmic harmony!

happiness

A closet is a closet is a closet.
It's what we do with the closet that makes all the difference!

I see a harmonious flow
of timeless elegance
encapsulating my being . . .

I am grateful for another breath
of delicious, breathe-able air . . .

I am conscious of the cycle
of inspiration and harmonious
balance unfolding within . . .

Gratitude
is at the forefront
of each new day . . .

I see my true inner self
radiating with lightness
and genuine joy . . .

I am grateful
for the aromatics
nourishing my being . . .

I am conscious of
harmony's rhythmic flow ...

I am grateful for
my special gifts . . .

I am conscious of
the change I seek . . .

I am thankful for
this ah-ha moment . . .

My approach is interwoven
with appreciation . . .

I am grateful for the
next step of the journey . . .

JOY

breathe

Everything you need is at your fingertips.
Just reach!

I am grateful for another day
to live, laugh, love with zest . . .

Just
breathe . . .

I embrace heavenly delight
as I rediscover treasures
from days gone by . . .

With each breath
I give thanks
to the next step of the journey . . .

I celebrate
with joyful appreciation
the gift of life . . .

I see,
I feel,
I breathe . . .

Happy thoughts
flourish . . .

I am grateful for
blissful happenings
that blossoms along the way . . .

I feel the joy radiating
from within . . .

I am living the life
I dreamed of . . .

Positive chi radiates
as I recall our special time together . . .

I consciously breathe in
the transformative benefits
of feel-good emotions . . .

PASSION

I am conscious of my thoughts, the passion, and the desire
that manifest my creations!

As with all thing in life,
it begins with the planting of a seed.

I embrace
the splendor of my imagination
that manifests creativity. . .

I walk on earthy paths
of unadulterated soil . . .

I am conscious of
my passion that . . .

I am conscious of
the jubilant change
I seek . . .

I am conscious of
the shimmering sunlight
dancing around,
above, and through me . . .

It's what I do
with my thoughts
that make all the difference . . .

I love with
uplifting passion . . .

I treasure
each delightful memory
that pops into my mind . . .

What memories
make my heart
beat faster . . .

A new seed =
a new life . . .

I am aware of my passion
for radiant energy
and continuity . . .

I am planting a hardy seed
with intention to manifest
a timeless remembrance . . .

AWARENESS

hope

As I breathe in the transformative benefits of feel-good emotions, I manifest happy thoughts.

I am grateful for
my Eco-Conscious awareness . . .

With mindfulness
I raise my vibration . . .

I am conscious of
what I breathe, touch, hear,
and how I feel . . .

An eco-conscious lifestyle is
a necessity, not a luxury . . .

Each time I gaze into a thought,
a past memory surfaces . . .

I have a heightened sense
of my journey . . .

Creative thoughts
are abundant . . .

With each breath
I breathe in hope . . .

I increase the fluidity
of awareness
through my senses . . .

I am enlightened to
the energy that glows
within my being . . .

I am conscious of my holistic space
inspired by nature
that supports
inner and outer beauty + well-being . . .

I see with
conscious awareness
what is before me . . .

love

To transform a blank canvas, a single object,
into a living, breathing picture
is an injection of euphoria!

I write with intention
to manifest my inner light . . .

I see the tiny bud
soundlessly open
in full splendor . . .

I am conscious of
my desires that . . .

As I write, I empower myself
with heartfelt thoughts of . . .

I visualize my intention
and believe . . .

I love dangling lights and
crystal jewels for
therapeutic and playful purposes . . .

I believe in
the manifestation of
my intention . . .

My special haven reflects
an Eco-Conscious,
Healthy-Living Lifestyle . . .

Thoughts crystalize
as I become aware . . .

I willingly manifest
happy belief thoughts . . .

As my intention manifests,
my inner light shines . . .

To see my thoughts
expressed on paper
provides clarity concerning
the person I have become . . .

LOVE

embrace

Whether you see it in the open or behind a
closed door it is always on display!

I am pulling it all together
with love and purpose . . .

I embrace a picturesque view of nature
while nature quietly
takes hold of me . . .

I live with
uplifting passion . . .

I embrace
my intentions
with clarity . . .

Lighthearted memories
flourish with ease . . .

I am essential
and have value . . .

I am forever fascinated
beyond the window . . .

I willing embrace
my personal story . . .

Inspiration and joy
encapsulate my being . . .

I embrace sweet visions
of uplifting, colorful emotion . . .

I am gratefully inspired
by my personal keyword
reference guide . . .

I welcome each new day
with joyful emotions of . . .

Create a mini-keyword reference guide of fantastical words. Personalize with categories, dates, and color code. Add new favorites that come your way.

Happy, Healthy Fantastical Words Please!

About the Author

Charisse Marei is an eco-conscious interior designer and "authorpreneur" who empowers and inspires people from all walks of life. As a passionate advocate for a healthy, eco-living lifestyle, she focusses on transforming interiors into beautiful, breathe-able dwellings combining her formal training in building biology, green design, feng shui, and essential oils with her passion for infusing harmony and balance, inspiration and purpose.

She is a graduate of Philadelphia College of Textile & Science and the International Institute for Building-Biology & Ecology, and had careers in interior and aviation design before launching her successful boutique design consultancy. She is the visionary, creative director, and illustrator of her work, including two books: *The Bathroom*, the first book in the series One Room at a Time: Your Essential Guide to a Beautiful Eco-Conscious, Healthy-Living Lifestyle, and *A Timeless Keepsake*. She is the creator of the ChaCha bracelet and ChaCha Mini Gem bracelet, designed to unify and empower women around the world, and of the lifestyle website Charisse Marei.

Her home is nestled in the beautiful rolling hills of Pennsylvania, where she lives with her husband, Dr. Drew, and "The Girls," Sage and Citrus, their two bichons frises. She is a daughter, sister, mother, and ChaCha to her seven grandchildren.

Her best days are sent working in her studio alongside "The Girls."

Learn more at charissemarei.com

FriesenPress

Suite 300 - 990 Fort St
Victoria, BC, V8V 3K2
Canada

www.friesenpress.com

ISBN
978-1-946414-15-1 (Hardcover)
978-1-946414-01-4 (Paperback)
978-1-946414-09-0 (eBook)

1. HOUSE & HOME

Distributed to the trade by The Ingram Book Company

CPSIA information can be obtained
at www.ICGtesting.com
Printed in the USA
BVHW02s0009030418
512291BV00002B/3/P